grey skies

Kaleigh Goldbey

BookLeaf Publishing

grey skies © 2022 Kaleigh Goldbey

All rights reserved.

No part of this publication may be reproduced, stored in a retrieval system, or transmitted, in any form or by any means, electronic, mechanical, photocopying, recording or otherwise, without the prior written permission of the presenters.

Kaleigh Goldbey asserts the moral right to be identified as author of this work.

Presentation by *BookLeaf Publishing*

Web: www.bookleafpub.com

E-mail: info@bookleafpub.com

ISBN: 9789357213974

First edition 2022

*To Mom, Nan, Lee, Matt & Kayleigh -
thank you for always believing in me.*

ACKNOWLEDGEMENT

Without my supportive family, loving partner and bestfriend in whole world - this book wouldn't be possible. Without you, individually but also collectively, I wouldn't be able to express some of these emotions in the way I do. We hit every low point together but celebrated all of the wins together too. I wouldn't be here, both physically and spiritually, without each of you.

PREFACE

My entire life, from as far back as I can remember, mental health has always been something I've struggled with. Through time, acceptance and giving myself the chance to make mistakes - I've learnt how to handle the ups and downs of my life while living with something that already feels unbearable. Little by little, with kindness towards myself and others, I've managed to numb the pain somewhat and now, the illness struggles with me. This book reflects that journey, and if it helps just one person make that journey to acceptance themselves then every tear I've ever cried, it was worth it.

grey skies

grey skies rolled over the hills
bringing darkness and turmoil
like a tsunami over an island

except i am the island

water consumes every piece
of rock and greenery
holding it under water until it suffocates
foundations begin crumble
roots and vines of every tree will scream
unheard - with water logged breath

except i am the island

innocent bystanders will stare
thankful to their god
that they, themselves, are out of the current
but lives will be lost the day the water comes
they'll stand on the shores, fearful
as the waves advance on the horizon

except i am not the island, i am the tsunami

31/03/09

my skin feels tight across my chest
like each side is pulling against each other
and trying to expose my aching heart
that is beating erratically out of sync

i'm drowning in non-existent tides
being held under by hands of other children
who, right now, do not understand
the implications of their schoolground chants

but eventually, they will know
when they post my mom's favourite school picture
up on the whiteboard in the assembly hall
and tell all the students i'm not coming back

eventually, they will know
when every facebook comment is discovered
read aloud in the playground,
and the bully, becomes the bullied

eventually, they will know
when their children come home
coughing up the same water from their lungs
that once, almost carried me away

i cling onto my aching chest
try to remember how to breathe
slumped against the girl's cubicle door
and whisper to myself, eventually, they will
know

and eventually, it will stop

black boots

guilt washed over me like an ocean
the waves exist, solely to become a hoarder
collecting grains from every single beach
until there is nothing left on every border

burnt toast that morning
finally sends me over the edge
but my loved ones all rush
to pull me back down from the ledge

monday mornings are the hardest
as i lay awake in bed
locked up in a prison cell
that only exists inside of my head

this sudden sense of loss
is just too much to bear
because it brings back all the feelings
i don't know how to share

your reasoning, a simple sentence
'they'll turn up, probably just misplaced'
but the real story, is harder to explain
even whispering the words, leaves a nasty taste

i couldn't tell you the truth
there were things i can't bring myself to say
so on the spot, i create a story
… well i lost my shoes today

room 201

through the glass doors and on straight ahead
keep going until the floor goes from white to red
where the caffeinated teachers, who are covered in paint
become an outcasted teenager's patron saint

but charcoal fingertips will make you a target
and blood doesn't show, on a red stained carpet
seek the teacher's gaze, but they won't meet your eye
and parents believe teachers because a teacher wouldn't lie

i tried to tell the truth, why i no longer go
but it's hard to explain the story when the bruises do not show
so the years continued by, and the grade got even lower
and every second period, the time went a little slower

until it was finally time, to pick an unwanted option
only one ingredient left, to make a toxic concoction

parents could see i had the talent
i thought that would grant me a pass

'i hope you aren't taking art
as i won't accept you in my class'

20:30:00 PM

my toast landed on the buttered side
and finally, i cracked

no longer could i squash the anger
inside of my brain, and keep up this charade
of pretending

pretending that i'm not angry
pretending that my choices weren't taken from me
living like i'm not in a permanent state of grief

grief for a loss that lives so deep
inside of my very being
that i'm attending my own funeral
and i'm awake inside of my coffin

smiling and comforting others
while i'm mourning for the loss
of the girl i should have been
that i will never get to meet

i am sad
but not the kind of sad that disappears
when the sun comes up and friends are around,
not the kind of sad that disappears

when the christmas sun peaks,
and spills into your bedroom

no i am sad
the kind that mixes with the atoms of your blood
and drowns your lungs when you lie awake at night
desperate to get, even 2 minutes sleep

no i am the kind of sad,
that when my toast lands
on the buttered side
i cry out for every little thing
that has crushed my lungs that day
for apologies i did not hear
for words i could not say

my toast landed on the buttered side,
and the screams finally became audible
peaking the ears, of my ill-informed mother
and she held me in her arms
on the cold tiled floor
and i told her i was mourning

i was mourning
the vacant lot
where her daughter used to lived
which has now been condemned
by the owner

missing piece

smoke filled the air around us
blurry bodies cramped together
between 4 metal posts, a barrier
like the one i could sense had been brewing
between us for a while

the music was deafening
yet the night seemed quiet
quieter than it had been inside of my head
for a while

she seemed different in this light
younger, yet older, simultaneously
the years hadn't been kind to either of us
yet somehow, she thrived

blossoming under the toxicity of pressure,
while i withered in the same garden
not popular, but still, not an outcast
with potential friends abundant

yet it was i, she gravitated too
like a comforter to a child
stuck in the war-torn city
that was our school environment

we agreed it was our shared trauma
and also our shared name
that bonded us, all those years
but now, even that seemed strained

until finally, she reached forward
clutching onto my hand,
blood rushing in my ears, she muttered words
i had dreaded to hear for years

you are my best friend
my best friend in the whole world
yet for years i feared you
that the phone would ring
and your mother would cry
she would tell me that you are gone
that your heart gave out
that you finally gave up

she cried

each tear landing on my skin
burning into my flesh
like acid searing into me
in that moment i realized

this pain didn't just torment my being

it tormented those around me
it seeped out of my pores
and infected every person
who got too close

like a plague in my brain
that only i could see

white

the guilt was beginning to eat me alive
but a small white packet
in the back of the cupboard
seemingly, numbed the pain

for the first time in months
a monster of a migraine
released its sharp grip from my skull,
that was almost cracking beneath its hand

a handful each day seemed enough
to keep the monster at bay
until little by little,
a handful turned into two

i found myself freefalling
into a nightmare
surrounded by monsters
much worse than those i'd already faced

these monsters had a grip on my soul
that was harder to fight
than i had ever had to battle before,
but this time i'm weaponless and alone

i'm silenced by embarrassment
isolated through shame,
the meds aren't working
and now my fingers are searching aimlessly

 seeking something stronger

clipboards & cocaine

my aimless search in the dark
had struck gold in a place
where gold should never lay
those wandering hands of mine
had grappled in the dark
playing tug of war against my better judgement

the lady with the clipboard
she says it's natural
to seek comfort in things that harm us
we don't see the dangers in our actions
at the time, there is no danger
because self-preservation doesn't exist

humans are a species like any other,
they will run or fight with things that hurt us
but people like me
we face danger head on
with a smile on our face and adrenaline in our hearts
because danger brings feeling

something our kind lack - is feeling
our souls are burdened with a fork in the road
a road of emptiness, a road of sorrow

the lady with the clipboard
she says we don't get to make the choice
of which road to take
that decision has already been made

i resist her analysis of who i am
i cannot be the only one who feels
both emptiness and sorrow
living as one inside of my soul

no i cannot be the only one
who feels like a puppet
strung up - lifeless yet performing
possessed by something, i cannot explain

yet, danger offers me a hand
and that hand holds a knife
urging me to cut my bindings and flee

but freedom doesn't come cheap

freedom comes half soaked in whiskey
with pockets, full of drugs
that fills the gaping hole in your soul
with a rag stuffed vodka bottle, then strikes a match

the lady with the clipboard
she says these decisions do not define us

that i don't decide these things
the chemicals inside of my head overrule all

i resist her analysis of who i am
because the voice in my head

it sounds just like me

hollow

the help they were supposed to give me
was like a pin-pricked egg right before dinner time
hollow and disappointing

the smoke that bellowed
out of the ashtray and into the air
filled my lungs but didn't numb the craving

no matter how many times
i tried to mend the void inside of my soul
it only seemed to grow emptier

everyone stands so sure of themselves
yet i grew smaller to hide
in a shadow of my former self

the help they promised
to battle the demons settling inside
the empty void of my being, barely left a scratch

my loved ones were still a long-awaited dinner
charming, fulfilling, and plentiful
and i, the pin pricked egg

00:00:01 AM

the tides had washed up
my broken and beaten body
onto the shores
and i was lost
barefoot with tender skin
and a hangover from hell

i'd finally managed to drag myself
out of the bed that had been covered in clothes
discarded, for weeks
with sheets so far past their sell by date
the smell of lavender had since long gone

it was the sound of familiar voices
that had finally tore me from a spiralling
nightmare
that no longer scared me
voices i hadn't seemed to hear for an eternity
the sound closely followed by a scent
unforgettable

my mother, she had finally had enough
she couldn't hold the ropes
that held her daughters shipwrecked soul alone
she was being submerged by waves

and she had to call in reinforcements

creaking floorboards almost gave the game away
but the monster that had held me for so long
gave me the skills to avoid detection
i had been creeping down these stairs
in the middle of the night for years

the voices were a frequency my tired ears
couldn't hear
but the closer to the door i got
less than an inch from being shut
i heard my family trying to build a life raft
made of carrier bags and disinfectant wipes

i had stumbled into a haphazard attempt
born out of desperation
where my closest loved ones
wore armour made of tin
and swords made of wood
unaware of what could possibly await them

but they were willing to follow me,
into battle

grippy socks

the battle had been fought
and this time, we won
but i knew a storm much stronger
was brewing on the horizon
and my loved ones had no shelter

they had already been soaked
down to the bone
by the clouds forming around me
and i decided it was time
to face the storm head on

i stepped out onto the battlefield
holding up a white flag
and retreated
the monsters were multiplying
the next battle, would be my defeat

i couldn't let my faithful battalion
fall beneath my crumbling weight
as i was slaughtered
by a monster
i had created

i was brave enough to face them

each time i was submerged
yet fearful enough to not fight back
so with every fibre inside of my body
i had one last act of bravery in me

i accepted their help

stitches

i haphazardly stitched
all my pieces back together
with different coloured thread
each time i fell apart

every colour, a visual
of emotions i felt
at each breaking point
of my life

so my being was made up
of shades, blue and green
like a wandering forest
next to the deepest ocean

shades of red and orange
for each time
anger ignited in my soul
like the fire that burnt, within

every so often
threads would come loose
and i dragged my trauma
behind me, like a cape

i thought, in my younger days
that this cape was a reminder
to myself, and others
that i will always be a craft

stitched together in haste
needing constant work
just to hold onto the threads
and i will never be perfect, off the shelf

but now i stand in front of the mirror
filled with nothing but colour
and accept myself
as just a work of art, in progress

yellow

green seemed to follow us everywhere we went
like the moon following the car
when you were a child

it was on every wall of the house
the front gate
even the cushions on the couch

it was the colour of the smoke
leaving your mouth
when you whispered in the cold

no matter the pigment, it reminded me of you
the tone in your eyes
and the smell on your clothes

every blade of grass
and newly budded flower that blossomed
had that hint, of you

when you left
green became grey
grey became sadness

i always preferred yellow anyway

03:00:00 AM

like a storm inside of a bottle
again, i was beginning to implode in on myself
my emotions, wild and cold

every waking moment
seemed to drag on for endless eternities
seconds felt like hours

the roots of my soul
fed into the ground like a tree looking for salvation
but was only met with poison

all forms of comfort felt rotten
like the taste of spinach in my mouth
forced onto me, as a child

i sought out any form of light
no matter how faint
i was trying to pull off that blindfold

but every word for help i tried to scream
felt like water invading my lungs
i was sinking further underwater than before

and i cannot swim

clique

i was already sinking
when i sat across that white desk
confronted by a person
who seemed to hate my being
the voices i had heard for years
those i'd finally escaped from
had now come back to haunt me
vicious hands held me down
tore open my chest
and began to dissect
the person i had fought to become
small sheets of black text sat between us
the deepest and darkest workings of my brain
spilled out onto that desk like a dictionary
melting in a house fire

she wanted me to explain
why the villain in these stories
always seemed to be her
yet she had been the wicked witch
with poison filled intentions
dragging me to her depths
and trying to steal my voice

but i had dealt with more ferocious villains than she
so the fairy-tale villain could never win
against the ones that resided
inside of me

bittersweet

with a little subtle glance
passion became burning desire

coffee stained post it notes
centred my entire world

rolling papers and staplers
stuck my broken heart back together

never before had i fell in love
with someone's posh phone voice

or a cup of tea at 9am
and the simple brush of a hand

but i'll never forget 12am confessions
of hidden emotions that sat behind a joke

the way you read my words on a page
and realised every word, to you they spoke

similar enough to know
that we'd never have been discreet

but completely different enough
that you eat my orange sweets

31/03/19

i pull out all my roots
and decide i no longer
want to plant myself
and remain stationery

no longer did i want
to hold myself down
inside a habitat
that was uninhabitable

the air was toxic
the soil was poisoned
my leaves withered
and flowers never grew

i wrapped my roots up
around my stem
and carried myself away
to flourish

to flourish
in my self-made sun
hand crafted soil
and crystal clear waters

slowly, the petals
poked through, into small buds
blooming into large flowers
and out, as vivid bright colours

i discovered new things
about those petals
as i became my very own
garden of eden

05:00:00 AM

the night had never felt so familiar
until i realised the love for the darkness
stemmed from irrational fears
of being alone in the silence

once that realisation settled
every lamp inside of my house
flickered with the immense stress
of being on once night fell

i was soothed by burning embers
that fell from hand rolled cigarettes
and barely there candles
completely exhausted at the wick

i never had a side of the bed
that i chose to sleep on
as the middle kept my fears at bay
and the blankets protected me

however, when you came
everything began to unravel
and the warm presence from your newly found
side of the bed
brought in a new kind of comfort

i could reach out
and find solace in the curvature
your collarbones made as you slept
that stopped my racing heart

the way your eyes glimmered
against the moon peeking through the blinds
as you sleepily glanced at me
created a safety blanket of their own

the familiar smell
left behind against my sheets
was protection to my soul
even when you were gone

i managed to turn the lights off

strength

when i was eight
i was told i wasn't feminine
because i loved
the colour blue

when my sister was twelve
she was told
as a woman
this is what you do

when we were fifteen
we saw our mother
with a blemish on her face
that had a purple hue

when i was eighteen
i decided i was more
than being something
merely, of virtue

when i was twenty one
i rebelled the ideologies
of women that i saw
as untrue

because women
r e g a r d l e s s
are not here
to serve you

sunrise

i have always loved stars
but i always hated the darkness

but to get one without the other
would be near impossible

so in that moment i had to make a choice
lose something i love or lose the glow

confronting a phobia as simple as darkness
seemed, almost easy

hold up a flickering lamp and watch it fall back
like darkness was itself afraid of the light

i explained this theory to my mother
a realist, by nature

she comforted and held me
as she began to tell me a story

without the darkness, the stars wouldn't glow
in quite the same way, that made me fall in love

she smiled and told me the same was true for
myself
my darkness allowed me to grow into something
light

and with that, i seemed to be at peace
when i realised dark and light united

give people what they loved most, in this world

Milton Keynes UK
Ingram Content Group UK Ltd.
UKHW022012160823
426962UK00017B/531